POLAND

LANDSCAPES IN MINIATURE

Photographs
PAWEŁ JAROSZEWSKI

Wydawnictwo Andrzej Frukacz

Ex Libris

Galeria Polskiej Książki

The Birth of the State

Krzysztof Burek

OSTRÓW LEDNICKI • GNIEZNO • POZNAŃ

Historians have no doubt that the core of the Piast state, whose earliest recorded history dates back to the second half of the 10th century, was territory belonging to the Polanie tribe. It was situated in the central part of Wielkopolska. It was there that essential social and political changes were initiated and important decisions of great consequence were made. It was also there that Poland was born.

Ostrów Lednicki, the largest of the four islands on Lake Lednica, bore witness to the first hours of our national history. A large stronghold was built on this site. It was used as the seat of the ruler and after adopting the Christian faith it also played the role of a religious center.

After sailing through the lake and reaching the shore of this unique island, one cannot resist being overcome by emotions at the sight of the remains of the centuries-old architecture. The chapel and the palladium evoke the images of the times of Mieszko. For over one hundred and fifty years these structures have been objects of interest of archaeologists and architecture historians. A dozen years or so ago, archaeologists discovered two characteristic hollows in the ancient floor of the chapel, dating from before 966. They are baptisteries connected with the small adjoining building considered to have been a bishop's residence (*episcopium*).

It can be assumed that here, on the Island of Ostrów Lednicki, on Holy Saturday in 966, the baptism ceremony of Prince Mieszko I and his court took place.

We stand silent facing the substantial evidence of that breakthrough event in the history of Poland, when the water of baptism was sprinkled on our native land for the first time. That is where the Christian era in the history of the Polish people began more than one thousand years ago. The heir of that history, the generation of the Third Republic of Poland, erected a metal construction over those holy relics. This is the Gate to the Third Millennium. It is shaped like a fish – a symbol of Jesus Christ. In June 1997, a helicopter carrying Pope John Paul II flew over it. The young people gathered on Ostrów Lednicki listened eagerly to the words of the Pope. He encouraged them to preserve the heritage of their ancestors and to make their lives in the Third Millennium based on the tenets of religion, hope and love. The young people answered that appeal by repeating the baptismal oath. Those were the same words uttered on that site by the first historic ruler of Poland, "in the name of the Father, and the Son and the Holy Ghost."

Setting out from Ostrów Lednicki, a place which enjoys the status of a national symbol, we begin our wandering to many other places in our homeland, such as Gniezno and Poznań, where reminders of our historical and cultural identity have been preserved. These relics of the past are part of our heritage, which we contribute to the mainstream of the restored unity of Christian Europe.

Lech's Mountain, a historic spot, is connected with the early days of statehood and of Christianity in Poland. Dominating the top of the hill are the towers of the Archcathedral Basilica, dedicated to the Assumption of the Holy Virgin Mary and to St. Adalbert. The interior of the church is Gothic. The pilasters and the ribs of the vaulting are made of sandstone. The focal point inside is the altarpiece with a silver reliquary made in 1662 by Peter van der Rennen, a goldsmith from Gdańsk.

The Renaissance Town Hall, a late 16th-century building, was designed by Giovanni Battista Quadro.

The Działyński Palace – its neoclassical façade dates from the second half of the 18th century. The figure of a pelican at the top symbolizes the resurrection of Poland after the years of captivity.

The history of the Archcathedral Basilica dedicated to the Apostles Saint Peter and Saint Paul dates back to the 10th century. The church, consisting of an ambulatory and two aisles surrounded by chapels, is topped with several towers. Two main ones are 62 meters tall; three minor ones are the so-called lanterns. The Golden Chapel is a particularly precious part of the interior. It is a mausoleum of Mieszko I and King Bolesław the Brave.

The National Sanctuary is a place of special worship of St. Mary in Poland. The internal chapel houses the venerated picture of Our Lady of Częstochowa (14th century). The interior of the church is adorned with stucco--work and murals by K. Dank-wart.

The ruins of a 14th-century Gothic and Renaissance castle, one of the many castles on the Trail of the Eagles' Nests.

* * *

The castle is situated over the Prądnik Valley in the Ojców National Park. The edifice dates from the 14th century. The Renaissance castle was originally Gothic.

The Vistula River, often called the Queen of the Polish rivers, has its sources somewhere on the slopes of the Silesian Beskid Mountains, among the spruces of the Mt Barania Góra Nature Reserve. The thickest of one of the most precious spruce forests in Europe, known as the so-called Istebna species, hide the sources of the Czarna Wi and the Biała Wisełka, whic their waters with the broo Roztoczny and Wątrobny. I town of Wisła both the Czarn

and the Biała Wiselka form iver – the Little Vistula – whose rs flow on getting mightier mightier. For a number of uries, the Vistula River Val-

ley constituted a commercial trail that ran from the Carpathian foothills to the Baltic Sea, connecting small villages and renowned cities situated near the river.

The ornamented façades of old townhouses, numerous nooks and crannies, church towers and the Renaissance ornaments of the Cloth Hall contribute to the charming and unique character of the Market Square in Kraków, which is one of the largest city squares in Europe. It is surrounded with a regular network of streets. Only one of them, leading to Wawel Hill is oblique. The southern corner of the Square is dominated by the sky-reaching towers of St. Mary's Church while the opposite corner by the Gothic Town Hall Tower. Near the outlet of Grodzka Street, the Market is closed with a small edifice of St. Adalbert's – a Romanesque church, which for centuries has been standing on this spot – once a junction of commercial trails.

The present luster of the interior of St. Mary's Basilica is a result of the comprehensive restoration works carried out during the last ten years. The colorful murals are the work of Jan Matejko. Together with his two students, Stanisław Wyspiański and Józef Mehoffer, he created the new, 19th-century interior decorations. At the same time Tadeusz Stryjeński, an architect, restored the former Gothic character to the church. However, he managed to preserve the works of art which accumulated there throughout the previous centuries. The arches of the side chapels make the space of the church dynamic and they direct one's attention to the chancel, where a crucifix is suspended in the rood-screen, under the blue vault, adorned with golden stars. The light assumes the colors of the stained-glass windows, closing the 14th-century chancel. The focal point of the church is an altar created by master Veit Stoss. It is truly a sculptural masterpiece. The altar, belonging to the largest pentaptychs in Europe, presents the life of St. Mary – the patron Saint of the church. The sculpted story begins with the presentation of Her family-tree and is concluded with the scene of Our Lady's coronation. This monumental work of art was created in the years 1477–1489 and it forever linked the name of its creator, Veit Stoss, with Kraków.

The Market Square in Kraków has for centuries been the site of important events in the life of the City and of the Polish state. The history of the Cloth Hall began in the 13th century, when King Boleslaus the Chaste, in the charter of Kraków, dated 1257, promised to build the vending stalls in the city. Not long afterwards, in 1306, Ladislas the El-bow-high granted the privilege of storage to the city. Henceon, the traveling merchants were obliged to stop in Kraków and to sell their goods through the local vendors. In the years 1380–1400 the vending stalls were en-larged and in that way the Cloth Hall came into being. After a fire in 1555 it was rebuilt according to the Renaissance style by Gio-vanni Maria Padovano. The ed-ifice was given its final shape by Tomasz Pryliński, an archi-tect who was in charge of its res-toration at the end of the 19th ce tury. Like in the past, all day lo the Cloth Hall is alive with act ity and the vending stalls are v ited both by Cracovians a tourists. When dusk falls a with the onset of silence, filigree arcades and the dai elements of the Renaissance tic bathe in darkness; it alm seems that the old walls s spinning stories of the mercha of old...

Arcades decorate the yard of Collegium Maius, the oldest building of the Jagiellonian University in Cracow. Queen Jadwiga, devoted to the idea of renovating the university founded by King Casimir the Great in 1364, donated her funds, jewels and clothes for this purpose. Year 1400 marked the beginning of the University's golden years. Its graduates include Nicolaus Copernicus, Jan Kochanowski, King John III Sobieski, and many generations of men of letters and science. The University later acquired new buildings, including Collegium Novum, a neo-Gothic building designed by Feliks Księżarski.

The Wawel Castle, which Polish kings selected for their premises, was built on a limestone rock. The early settlements on Wawel Hill date back to the tenth cen-tury and the reign of King Bo-leslaus the Brave. Under the present-day castle, there are rem-nants of the Romanesque build-ings – the Rotunda of St. Felix and Audauctus. The Cathe towers overshadow the R Castle and the Renaissance y all surrounded by walls.

In the year 1000, a bishopric subject to the Metropolis of Gniezno was established in Kraków. The cathedral on Wawel Hill became the center of religious and state events. A Gothic church, with its three towers visible over the castle walls, was built there on the site of the early pre-Romanesque church. This was the place of coronations of Polish kings and also one of their biggest necropolises. Inside the cathedral, the numerous works of art constitute the testimonies of centuries gone by. There are sculpted and canopied sarcophagi of the rulers, altarpieces, murals and woodcarvings. The focal point is the shrine of St. Stanislaus the Bishop, with the sepulcher and reliquary of the martyr.

Sandomierz: a town situated on seven hills around the Vistula River Valley, has been part of Polish history for ten centuries. It was the center of the province, formed already during the tribal era of Poland, which was dis- tinctly separated from the Cra- cow province – the other prov- ince in the Małopolska region. During the reign of the first kings from the Piast dynasty it was one of the country's capitals (*sedes regni principales*). During the time when the country was amongst the sons of the ceased King Boleslaus the mouth into numerous dis Sandomierz was the capital duchy, and later a large Voiv ship. It always remained a

religious life, a town with churches and monaster- nd from 1818 the seat of a se. There are few places in nd where in such a small one can see so many ob- of architecture and art, from Romanesque to the constructivism of the 1930s. Polish culture, science and spirituality would have been much poorer without the work of people related to Sandomierz. As Pope John Paul II said, 'a strange power has settled in this town, the source of which comes from the Christian tradition.'

One such mansion was built in Żelazowa Wola, not far from Sochaczew – the ancient town of the Mazovian dukes. In 1802, Nicolas Chopin arrived at such a mansion in Żelazowa Wola. Miss Justyna Krzyżanowska, a relative to the Skarbek family, happened to live in the house. Days spent under one roof ig-nited the flame of mutual a tion. On June 2, 1806, in monumental Renaissance p. church in Brochów (whic one of the very few Polish c

that was built as a fortress) was wedded Justyna. Almost later, on April 6, 1807, first-Ludwika came into the ; and three years later, on February 22, 1810, Fryderyk was born.

Among the capitals of Central Europe ranging from Bucharest, Budapest and Prague to Copenhagen, it is the history of Warsaw that will rouse horror, compassion and, finally, admiration in a scrupulous researcher. Like an inn, difficult to defend on the crossing of international roads, Warsaw was burned, ransacked and demolished over the centuries by the armies which incessantly marched through it (...).

Jerzy Waldorff

The reconstruction of the Royal Castle, which was completely destroyed during World War II, took many years. At present it is again a prominent icon of Polish identity and its cultural symbol. Next to the castle is the Old Town, which in the summer of 1944 was an insurgents' redoubt. It was carefully rebuilt from the destruction it suffered during the war. It is now an attractive place for both the inhabitants of Warsaw and for visitors. There are numerous restaurants, cafés, galleries and souvenir shops. It gets silent and empty only in winter time after dusk.

The Old Town in Warsaw is surrounded by a ring of the former city walls. The little tenement houses, standing wall to wall with each other, line the streets demarcated centuries ago. Above their red roofs soar the towers of churches, the Royal Castle and a high column with the statue of the king who made this city in Mazovia the capital of the Republic of Poland. Not so long ago, the place was marked with insurgents' graves on which candles were burning.

The old Warsaw cemetery is like a huge book describing two hundred years of the difficult fame and glory of the capital, so fatally situated on the European crossroads. It does not matter if these pieces of history are important with regards to public or personal matters. Walking from one grave to another is like turning over the pages of this great book, forwards or backwards, meeting unexpected events or people, standing in awe of their portraits so unlike our imagination might dictate if we knew the histories of lives of the deceased.

Jerzy Waldorff

The interior of the Cathedral was illuminated for the celebration of the holy orders in 1999. The walls are richly ornamented with neo--Romanesque murals painted in the years 1904–1914 by Władysław Drapiewski.

In the medieval City of Toruń, the most distinguished church was the Cathedral Basilica dedicated to two saints – John the Baptist and John the Evan-gelist. The construction of the church began in 1270. It was subsequently re-edified in the 14ᵗʰ and the 15ᵗʰ centuries. At present its form is that of a three-aisled basilica surrounded l ring of chapels. A monumer 52-meter tall tower, adorned v the gilded dial of a clock, o looks the narrow streets.

ch is surrounded with lux-
nt trees. On the top of the
er, its mighty 4-meter thick
s hide the famous medieval
the *Tuba Dei*, cast in 1500.

The interior is illuminated with
colorful beams of light passing
through the stained-glass windows above the main altar. The
late-Gothic triptych of St. Wolf-

gang, dating from about 1502, is
situated in this prominent place.

Toruń welcomes visitors with the towers of a medieval town hall and with the brick walls of the stronghold of the Teutonic Knights. The city was developed on the site of the former settlement, which was situated near the ford on the Vistula River, on the commercial trails leading from Hungary to Ruthenia and to Western Europe. From the first half of the 13th century the area was under the rule of the Order of Teutonic Knights. The city belonged to the Hanseatic League and in 1403 it was granted the privilege of storage. Thus it began to compete with Gdańsk and Kraków. The year 1454 in Toruń saw the outbreak of an uprising against the Teutonic Knights. After the end of the Thirteen Years' War, as a result of the Treaty of Toruń, the city was returned to Poland.

The Gothic Town Hall in Toruń, one of the most beautiful ones in Poland, is situated in the middle of the Market Square. It was built on the shape of a quadrangle and it incorporated the buildings of the Cloth Hall, the Bread Stalls, the Town Tower and the Weigh House. Numerous modernization works carried out here brought about some architectural additions, such as the tower, the stories, the gables and the corner turrets. The charm of the Medieval, late-Gothic architecture survived in the nooks crannies of Toruń. There numerous tiny tenement hou granaries, as well as fragm of city walls and defensiv wers.

ń is the birthplace of Nico-
Copernicus (1473). His mo-
ent has a prominent place in
Market Square, in the vicinity
e Town Hall. Copernicus'
se, with a painted façade, has
preserved until today.

Malbork, a Teutonic fortress on the bank of the Nogat River, was one of the most magnificent defensive structures in Europe in the Middle Ages. Throughout the history of the independent Teutonic state, the castle was the headquarters of the Teutonic Order. The construction of the castle began around 1278, as the new headquarters of the Commander of the Order, who was then abandoning its former residence in the nearby town of Zantyr. The building was erected on the peninsula surrounded with the flood waters of Żuławy (the Vistula Warpland) and the Nogat River. Its high walls were surrounded with moats, while drawbridges hindered access to the castle gates. The stronghold is divided into the High Castle and the Middle Castle.

Gdańsk cityscape – a view across the Motława.

The mighty bell-tower of St. Mary's Church, topped with a crown of spires, rises high over the roofs of Gdańsk. St. Mary's basilica is the largest Gothic church in Poland and the largest of the brick Gothic churches in Europe. It can hold up to 25,000 people. The three-aisled basilica dating from 1343 was enlarged in the years 1372–1502. It was given the form of a huge, spatial hall with high windows to let in light. The main altarpiece, *St. Mary's Coronation*, dating from 1517, is a work of Master Michael of Augsburg. The space above the chancel is closed off by a group of sculptures situated on the rood-screen beam. It is entitled *The Crucifixion* and dates back to 1517. From 1507 till the end of WWII, St. Mary's was a protestant church. In 1992 it became a co-cathedral of the metropolis of Gdańsk.

The former Cistercian church – the Archcathedral Basilica dedicated to the Holy Trinity – is situated in the nearby district of Gdańsk Oliwa. The most splendid showpiece inside is the Baroque organ, a masterpiece of the organ-builder Jan Wulf of Orneta. The instrument was constructed from 1763 to 1788 and then rebuilt in 1934. At present it has almost 8 thousand pipes. The magnificent, high altar in St. John's church is made of stone. It is the only such work of art in Europe. Sculpting it took Master Abraham van dem Block thirteen years (1599–1612). The ornaments include the scenes depicting the Last Supper and the Passover, as well as the effigy of Christ in Jerusalem. The altar survived the total destruction of the church as well as the fire in 1945.

The Long Market, the central place of old Gdańsk, is closed off from the east by the Green Gate – a grand palace going back to 1568. It was built by Jan Kremer who thus fulfilled the commission received from the Municipal Council. By building that palace the burghers of Gdańsk wanted to express their gratitude to King Casimir Jagiellon for liberating them from under the domination of the Teutonic Order.

The Łeba Sandbar is a narrow stretch of a sandy land between Lake Łebsko and the open sea. It features a desert-like landscape and it is even referred to as the "Polish Sahara." The ridge of dunes, almost 20 kilometers long, occupies almost the entire width of the Łeba Sandbar. The picturesque landscapes change constantly under the influence of winds. The dunes move in a wavelike way, taking fantastic shapes and forms. In the places where the winds are particularly intensive, the dunes can move inland up to several meters a year. That is why they are called shifting dunes. The sands of the Słowiński National Park resemble a real desert so much, that the armored Africa Corps used the area as a training-ground before their operations in Africa.

The Łeba Sandbar is a narrow stretch of a sandy land between Lake Łebsko and the open sea. It features a desert-like landscape and it is even referred to as the "Polish Sahara." The ridge of dunes, almost 20 kilometers long, occupies almost the entire width of the Łeba Sandbar. The picturesque landscapes change constantly under the influenc winds. The dunes move wavelike way, taking fant shapes and forms. In the p where the winds are particu

sive, the dunes can move
d up to several meters a
That is why they are called
ng dunes. The sands of the
iński National Park resemble a real desert so much, that
the armored Africa Corps used
the area as a training-ground before their operations in Africa.

Ostrów Tumski, once an island in the Odra riverbed, is the historical cradle of Wrocław. As early as the 10th century, the first residence of the Duke was established here and several years later a bishop's dwelling was built next to it. The location of the settlement was exceptionally good, since the river surrounding it made it a safe place. At the same time the nearby commercial trail contributed to its growing wealth. At present Ostrów Tumski is a symbol of the earliest history of Wrocław. From the waters of the Odra River emerges the silhouette of the island, with two churches – the collegiate of the Holy Cross and the two-towered cathedral dedicated to St. John the Baptist.

Gothic Town Hall, the Cloth and the numerous Renaise portals and façades of the ment houses are the testimo of the former prosperity. / fill any visitor of the Mar Square in Wrocław with ad tion. The Market owes its atmosphere and location to Prince Henry the Bearded who established his capital city here in the 13th century. The square, measuring 175 x 212 meters, inscribed in a regular network of streets, was established then. The life of the patriciate flourished around the Town Hall. The textile trade developed in the nearby Cloth Hall, while other craftsmen, such as cobblers, saddlers or goldsmiths, had their stalls in the neighboring buildings.

The Błędne Skały (the Erratic Boulders) constitute one of the greatest curiosities of nature in Poland. Covering an area of barely 21 hectares, the cracked sandstone rocks create a complex system of clefts and corridors and the numerous extraordinary stone formations have been arranged by Nature into a sculpture gallery. The shapes look so real that some specimens have even been given names – Rock Saddle, Mushroom, Gate. Every single glance cast at the rocks brings new associations into mind. The several-meter tall boulders have little support. Trees and bushes have managed to creep into the narrow crevices. Tiny pools of water reflect the scanty light that reaches the bottom of the labyrinth...

Trzy Korony (Mt Three Crowns) is a typical of the Pieniny Mountains. Its altitude is 982 meters. Visible from a distance, towering over a gentle mountain range, it consists of several tops which together form a picturesque group of rocks. Trzy Korony is situated in the Pieniny National Park that was originally established in 1930.

A panorama of the Tatras seen from a plane flying 2000 meters above ground evokes admiration with its diversity of rock formations – the soaring pikes, the snow-covered mountain-tops, the deep green valleys and the vast mountain pastures. The length of the Tatra range, measured along the ridge, is 80 kilometers. The highest mountain on the Polish side of the range is Mt Rysy, whose altitude is 2499 meters.

The sunrise over Lake Solina emphasizes the riches of the landscape – the distant mountain ranges and the diversified shoreline of the lagoon.

Today the Bieszczady is a mountainous border region in the south-eastern part of Poland. The gentle, wooded slopes of the mountains are crossed by countless streams and brooks. The highest ranges, with their grassy pastures, rise up to 1300 meters above sea level. In the past, the Bieszczady was considered to be the wildest area in Poland, while nowadays, it is visited by crowds of tourists and wanderers. In 1973, the Bieszczady National Park was established. It inco rates particularly precious picturesque mountain ran The natural reservations wi the Park constitute a "refuge the rare specimens of flora fauna. The thickets of the wo

are the habitat of the bear, wolf, the impressive Carian deer, the European bi- and a number of other rare ies of animals.

The gorges of the Bieszczady brooks are particularly beautiful places where a sense of the wild prevails. The Valley of the Solinka rises up steeply over the riverbed of the brook. Its slopes are overgrown with old, oddly-shaped trees. The "Blue Whirlpools" ("Sine Wiry") Nature Reserve consists of a riverbed section of the Wotlin Brook making its way among the boulders and through the landslides. The water has worked its way between the slopes of the valley and foams abundantly when falling over the numerous transverse steps.

Przemyśl

Przemyśl is a town whose panorama seems to have been designed by an eminent painter. The layout of the buildings on the slope of the San River Valley, on the very edge of the Carpathian hills, resembles a cascade. Church towers rise high above the roofs of the houses. The towers of the former Carmelite monastery rise the highest; those of the Greek Orthodox cathedral and of the Franciscan church are situated at a lower level; the towers of St. John the Baptist's cathedral are visible in the background. Perched on the slope of a hill, among the snow-covered trees, is the white tower of the Przemyśl castle built in 1340 on the site of an old stronghold which had existed there in the times of the Ruthenian dukes.

70

The Palace in Łańcut is the most magnificent of the residences preserved in south-eastern Poland. It was designed by Matteo Trapola, and built in the years 1629–1641, for Stanisław Lubomirski, a Ruthenian and Cracovian Voivode. The fourwinged palace with a courtyard, orangery and a library pavillion is surrounded by fortifications built in the shape of a five-armed star. Within the area of the residence, the owners created splendid garden arrangements. The alleys lead to the rose garden, the English-style garden, the Italian-style garden and the garden of perennial plants.

In 1661, a Grand Marshal and Crown Hetman, Jerzy Sebastian Lubomirski, had the palace restored for the wedding of his daughter Krystyna and Feliks Kazimierz Potocki.

The Bug River, which is of great importance in Polish history, flows majestically across a wide valley, meandering through broad meadows. Half way through its course it cuts through the Podlasie Region, a land which has been functioning as a bridge between the Christian traditions of the East and the West for centuries.

The Biebrza National Park covers 59 thousand hectares, and it is the last such area in Europe. The Valley of the Biebrza River changes its landscape according to the seasons, and is most beautiful in spring, when the river spreads onto surrounding meadows and pastures. The wildlife, untouched by industry and the expansion of man, hosts the original fauna and flora – the woods here are famous for the largest population of moose, waters are full of fish, an[d] moors are rich with turf p[...] When water rises in spring meadows fill with the soun[d of] birds – the moors are the [...] plentiful hatching area in Eu[...]

Hańcza, the deepest lake
)land (108.5 m), is a true
ler. This 5-kilometer long
everal-hundred-meter wide
is surrounded by steep
banks covered with rocks. Trees
bend over the still, dark waters,
and the rough rocky banks and
dark colours bear similarities to
northern-European lakes.

The peninsula on Lake Wigry was a place of seclusion and contemplation of the Cameldolite monks. The monastery founded by King Ladislaus IV was constructed on the hill on the peninsula, which offers a magnificent panorama of the lake. The hermit huts (erem were erected on terraced sl(and the monastery is don ed by the Church of the Im

e Conception. After World II the monastery buildings tioned as an arts and crafts er. The only centers of her-

mit life of the Cameldolite monks are the monasteries in Kraków and at Bieniszewo.

Publisher:

Ex libris

Galeria Polskiej Książki Sp. z o.o.

04-187 Warszawa - Poland
Dęblińska 13
tel. (022) 610-85-95, fax (022) 612-02-86
e-mail:exlibris@exlibris-pl.com
www.exlibris-pl.com

Photographs & the Concept of the Album:
PAWEŁ JAROSZEWSKI

Introduction:
KRZYSZTOF BUREK

Translation:
MAŁGORZATA WALCZAK, JUSTYNA PIĄTKOWSKA, EWA BASIURA, Letterman Ltd.

Proofreading:
ALAN WALCZAK, CHRIS HOWARD, JULIE SOKOL.

The text by Jerzy Waldorff is quotation from his earlier publication
and was included upon the author's approval and his selection.
„Za bramą wielkiej ciszy" Wydawnictwo Interpress 1990

Graphic design:
PaArt/ look STUDIO

DTP:
look STUDIO
Kraków , ul. Wielopole 17
tel./fax (012) 429-18-31, e-mail look@kki.pl

Printed by: DRUK-INTRO S.A. Inowrocław

This book is an abbreviated version of a larger album POLAND — THROUGHOUT THE CENTURII
TOWARDS THE NEW MILLENNIUM", published by "EX LIBRIS" Galeria Polskiej Książki Sp. z o.o.

ISBN 83-88455-14-1
ISBN (USA) 1-928900-05-4